*Well-behaved women
seldom make history.*
—LAUREL THATCHER ULRICH

Judy Blume

KATHLEEN KRULL

interior illustrations by
David Leonard

BLOOMSBURY
NEW YORK LONDON NEW DELHI SYDNEY

∼◌∼

To Emily Easton,
a woman who breaks the rules

∼◌∼

First published in the United States of America in June 2015
by Bloomsbury Children's Books
www.bloomsbury.com

Bloomsbury is a registered trademark of Bloomsbury Publishing Plc

For information about permission to reproduce selections from this book, write to
Permissions, Bloomsbury Children's Books, 1385 Broadway, New York, New York 10018
Bloomsbury books may be purchased for business or promotional use. For information on bulk purchases please contact
Macmillan Corporate and Premium Sales Department at specialmarkets@macmillan.com

Library of Congress Cataloging-in-Publication Data
Krull, Kathleen, author.
Women who broke the rules : Judy Blume / by Kathleen Krull ; illustrated by David Leonard.
pages   cm
ISBN 978-0-8027-3796-0 (paperback) • ISBN 978-0-8027-3795-3 (hardcover)
1. Blume, Judy. 2. Authors, American—20th century—Biography. I. Leonard, David, illustrator. II. Title.
PS3552.L843Z745 2015   813'.54—dc23   [B]   2014012065

Art created with Acrylic
Typeset in Beaufort
Book design by Nicole Gastonguay

Printed in China by Leo Paper Products, Heshan, Guangdong
2 4 6 8 10 9 7 5 3 1 (paperback)
2 4 6 8 10 9 7 5 3 1 (hardcover)

All papers used by Bloomsbury Publishing, Inc., are natural, recyclable products
made from wood grown in well-managed forests. The manufacturing processes
conform to the environmental regulations of the country of origin.

TABLE OF CONTENTS

1 LITTLE MISS PERFECT

Like most kids, Judy Blume had a *lot* of questions.
Okay, maybe more than most kids. What she didn't have were answers. She grew up in a stifling time, when the rules stopped people from being honest and real.

Born on February 12, 1938, in Elizabeth, New Jersey, she had a close-knit family. Her dad was a dentist who took care of people's teeth. Her mom took care of Judy and her older brother, David. That's what many moms did then—stayed home. Each night the family ate dinner together. There was no TV then, so they listened to *The Shadow* and other radio shows, and went to the movies.

With her allowance money, every week Judy bought a book at the bookstore. After visits to the public library, she'd play Library when she got home, with herself as a tiny librarian. Her favorites were the Betsy-Tacy books by Maud Hart Lovelace, comforting stories about best friends growing up in a small town.

Which did she like better—books or boys? At six she was in love with not just one boy, but two (Jimmy and Tommy). In sixth grade she formed a club with her four best friends, called the Pre-Teen Kittens. Over Oreo cookies and Cokes, they compared notes on the changes in their bodies . . . and boys. Judy liked a different boy every week.

But Judy never got in trouble.

Her brother was the rebel (once, he kicked his kindergarten teacher in the stomach). She felt she had to be the opposite: "I was Little Miss Perfect." Her relationship with her parents was fond but not honest. Basically, she told them what they wanted to hear: "I never felt that I could be sad or disappointed or even angry."

Her biggest crime, for which she was never caught, was writing reports on books she had invented. She just wasn't that interested in horse stories or books about little girls on the prairie.

Where were the books that talked about real family relationships, boys and girls, bodily changes, and racial prejudice?

And religion. Her Jewish family followed certain traditions but was not particularly religious. Her father had six brothers and sisters, most of whom died during Judy's childhood. Her family "was always sitting Shiva"—the weeklong Jewish tradition of mourning a close relative. Religion was so confusing.

And what about all her fears? Judy was afraid of lightning and thunder, vomit, sudden loud noises, dogs, and swimming. She worried that her father, whom she adored, would die young like his siblings. At night she bargained with God to keep her dad alive, making up prayers she'd repeat seven times a day.

"I wanted to read books about real life," she complained. "I always thought I was the only one and . . . I thought I was weird." But back then most parents avoided talking about personal stuff with their kids.

Inside, Judy felt herself becoming "a secret storyteller," making things up in her head: "Stories and stories and stories, but I never told anyone." She thought she might like to be a librarian, and she also dreamed about becoming a cowgirl, a detective,

a spy, a ballerina, and a movie star. In reality the careers open to her were nurse, teacher, airplane stewardess, and stay-at-home mom—which is what everyone expected her to become.

Being a writer seemed as unreal as one of her made-up stories: "I didn't know anything about writers. It never occurred to me they were regular people and that I could grow up to become one."

Judy went to an all-girls high school. Too bad, it didn't

have boys. But like many bold women, she later said this gave her confidence. Girls ran the show at her school.

She was always a good student. She worked on the school newspaper and kept a diary. She sang in the chorus, studied piano, and took modern dance. She adored dancing, but it was probably not going to work out as a career. Her toes had a weird way of making funny sounds on the stage—*crack! pop!* The other dancers would get the giggles.

But the older she got, the more boring she felt. She wished she had the "depth and curiosity" she'd had as a ten-year-old.

After graduating with high honors, she picked a college that was said to have cute boys.

After all, the average age women got married then was twenty.

Judy's first college was Boston University, but she soon had to leave after falling ill. When she was well again, she started over, this time at New York University in Greenwich Village. She was *cool*, part of the bohemian scene, with its poetry readings, folk music concerts, and sidewalk cafés. Trying to ditch the boring 1950s, she felt like a rebel. At school, she dared to wear turtlenecks and jeans (but switched back to her pastel skirt-and-sweater sets when she went home).

In 1960 she earned a degree in education, planning to

teach second grade. Instead she met a nice young man, got married, and had two children—a daughter, Randy, then a son, Larry, by the time she was twenty-five.

A career outside the home would have seemed weird. She didn't know one woman with a job. Judy adored her kids: "I loved taking care of them, but I was a little bit cuckoo, staying at home and not having a creative outlet."

At the same time as she felt she was going crazy, books were coming out about *other* women going crazy. It turned out a lot of them were tired of being second-class citizens. It was a whole new thing called women's liberation, a movement to free women from the old rules. "Everything changed," said Judy.

Some called it "women's lib" and made fun of women who took part in the demonstrations and activities. But the movement wouldn't be stopped. The 1960s were turning into a tidal wave of change.

Judy was thrilled. She bought the new *Ms.* magazine— for women who didn't want to use "Miss" or "Mrs." and be labeled according to whether or not they had a husband. Becoming *Ms.* Blume gave her courage, like having "my own little feminist movement inside me."

Judy began to feel that she needed to express herself. At first she tried writing songs. Then she made banners out of felt and sold them to department stores. Writing books for children was next. It just seemed natural: "I was in my twenties, but my experiences as an adult were limited. I identified more with kids than with the adults in my life."

Like many beginning children's book writers, she wrote only in rhyme, in imitation of Dr. Seuss. She admitted later that these first attempts were "really bad." She kept them locked in a box, and she has threatened to haunt her children if they ever publish them.

She took a class on writing for children and teens. The teacher laid out the rules. Stories should give lessons and end happily. They shouldn't leave loose ends or have more questions than answers. They should protect children from unpleasant reality.

Judy liked the class so much that she took it twice. But even then, she was thinking to herself, *I don't care about rules and regulations of writing for children.* She wanted to write what children's lives were truly like: "It's really hard to be a child, and no one has shown just how hard it is."

Other people didn't understand her. Not her husband, nor his best friend, an English major at college who told her, "You're a nice girl, Judy, but you can't write." She sent a manuscript to a published picture book writer and he said, "Give it up. You have no talent."

No way was she giving it up. She pounded away on her nonelectric typewriter while her children were in school. And she mailed out story after story to publishers along with her own amateurish colored-pencil drawings.

For two long years, all she received was rejections.

But still she persisted. This had become her dream—to be a published writer. At night she would say to herself, "I don't even care if they pay me. Just let me be published."

In the morning she'd feel better: "I'd wake up and say, 'I *can* do this.'" With each rejection, she felt herself getting a little stronger.

Judy Blume was *not* an overnight success. But eventually she sold two short stories. "The Ooh Ooh Aah Bird" and "The Flying Munchkins" each earned her twenty dollars. Her writing teacher bought her a red rose.

She couldn't stop now. Her first book, *You, Mom, You?*, got many rejections and was never published. Her next one was about a middle child who feels invisible until he gets to play a kangaroo in the school play. This time, a publisher rejected her bad drawings but did like her text. They wanted to publish her book! When she got the news, she picked up her kids and spun them around.

In 1969 *The One in the Middle Is the Green Kangaroo*

became her first published book. "Mom Keeps Busy Writing Books for Little Children" was the headline in her local paper. Everyone considered Judy's writing an amusing hobby.

With the $350 from that sale, she bought her first electric typewriter. She set to work on a novel for kids ages eight to twelve. The subject was daring for its time—an African American family moving into an all-white neighborhood. With *Iggie's House*, Judy was trying to show the realities of racial prejudice.

Just as she was finishing up, she saw an ad. A new publisher called Bradbury Press was looking for realistic novels for ages eight to twelve.

No one was more ready than Judy Blume.

3 IT'S ME, JUDY

With high hopes, she sent off *Iggie's House*.

Bradbury Press quickly accepted it, and published it in 1970.

At her first lunch with her editor, Judy tried to act cool. She cracked a lame joke about the waiter dropping something in her glass. The stuffy waiter pointed out that he put a lemon wedge in every water glass.

Her editor stopped taking her to fancy restaurants. He just wanted to talk about Judy's writing. They ate sandwiches together while going over her manuscripts in his office.

She was in heaven, writing novels with a real publisher encouraging her. She kept mastering her craft, rereading her favorite books from childhood, the Betsy-Tacy books. She was inspired by newer books like Louise Fitzhugh's *Harriet the Spy* and E. L. Konigsberg's quirky novel *From the Mixed-Up Files of Mrs. Basil E. Frankweiler*. Her biggest hero was Beverly Cleary.

"I fell off the couch laughing," she said of reading Cleary's

Ramona books—"I knew I wanted to write books like those."

She was on a roll. Over the next ten years, she published thirteen more books. The one that made her a star was *Are You There God? It's Me, Margaret*, in 1970. Margaret was a witty twelve-year-old girl coping with questions about religion, friendship, and the strange things that happen to our bodies as we grow up. There was no other book quite like it.

Some people raised their eyebrows. But then a rave review appeared in the *New York Times*, which later named the book one of the outstanding books of that year. Judy took this as proof: she really was a writer.

The following year she received her first fan letter—from a thirteen-year-old girl. Judy was so jazzed, she wrote back to her the very same day.

She plunged ahead. In 1971 she published two more novels. *Then Again, Maybe I Won't* is about many of the same things as her *Margaret* book, but from a boy's point of view. *Freckle Juice* is a funny book about a boy who so desperately wants freckles that he falls victim to a prank.

With *It's Not the End of the World*, she tackled the crushing effect of divorce on kids. Divorce was a topic barely whispered about, and it had never been treated in such a realistic way in a book for kids.

Divorce was heavy on Judy's mind, as she and her husband ending up getting one. At that time divorce was still rare, and for many, a source of shame. "What will I tell my friends?" said her mom. It was a time full of pain for Judy and her kids. She remarried too quickly, and that marriage also ended in divorce. "Anyone who thinks my life was cupcakes all the way is wrong," she said.

It was writing—about this and other thorny topics—that kept her going through her own tough times: "Did writing change my life? It totally changed my life. It gave me my life."

With *Tales of a Fourth Grade Nothing*, she introduced Peter Hatcher and his bratty, annoying little brother, Fudge. It is an intense portrait of sibling rivalry, but also very funny. "I enjoy nothing better than hearing a kid laugh while reading a book," she said.

Kids ate it up. Due to popular demand, she went on to use

some of the same characters in *Otherwise Known as Sheila the Great*, *Superfudge* (her all-time bestselling book), *Fudge-a-Mania*, and *Double Fudge*.

Judy considered *Blubber* to be her best book for young children. About a girl who stands up to a bully, it was popular but controversial. It exposed bullying in a more realistic and complex way than people were used to. It didn't wrap up in a nice tidy way—the main bully never gets punished.

One of Judy's trademarks was total honesty: "I wanted to be honest—maybe because I felt grown-ups hadn't been honest with me when I was a kid." Another trademark was that her girls were always as strong as her boys. They were feisty young feminists.

No matter what Judy's characters did, she never used a judgmental tone. Most of her books were told in the first person through the eyes of a kid. This allowed her to speak directly to readers in a way they immediately related to. She had an amazing ability to write how real kids talked.

So much to explore—parents not understanding their children, life being unfair, kids lacking power over their own lives.

She just wanted to tell stories, but she also wanted to help.

How did Judy accomplish so much? Part of it was sheer hard work—she tried to write seven days a week.

Like many writers, she kept a trusty notebook with her at all times. Before starting a book, she jotted down any little detail she could think of about the story.

Writing first drafts was truly "torture." But once she got something on the page and played with it, putting pieces together like a puzzle, the process became fun. Yet there was more work to be done. She usually wrote three drafts before sending something to an editor. Then another five drafts before the book was complete.

Her favorite part of the writing process was—what else?—finishing. "I wonder, *How did I do that?* because when you write you go off into that other part of your brain and it's as if you're not aware of writing."

After each book, she liked to do something completely different, which explains the variety in her works.

She refused to admit that so-called writer's block existed. She came to trust herself: "We all have some days that are better than others. If it's a bad day, if it just won't come, get up and walk around, do something else. Tomorrow it will come."

Movement was the cure. Her favorite remedies for a bad day were power walking, kayaking, and biking. A dancer, she took tap lessons for years.

Judy's least favorite part of writing was being alone: "You spend most of the day in a little room by yourself."

In fact, about ten books into her career, she seriously thought about quitting. The loneliness was getting to her. But in the end, she came to believe that "the freedom of writing" outweighed the job's lonely nature.

Besides, by then, her millions of loyal fans would have protested.

Her dream had come true in the most startling way. By 1982 Judy was the most popular children's author ever. Ten of her books were on the American Library Association's list of the top forty most popular books for children.

Kids were passing around her books in classrooms and on playgrounds. They found the books addictive, and they couldn't get enough. Judy spoke to kids as if she were an oracle, a guru to guide them through life. Kids flooded her with letters expressing their thanks and wanting her help with their own fears, doubts, and worries.

She was grateful, if a bit baffled: "I don't understand why I am so successful, except that there must be something I do that makes people see themselves in my stories."

Everyone loved Judy Blume.

Actually, not everyone.

No, it wasn't all cupcakes.

Some adults complained that Judy's books weren't "fine" literature; they weren't classics. No shiny Newbery Medals decorate any of her book covers, for example. Her books were accused of being like comfort food—candy with no nourishment. Some felt her writing was sloppy, choppy, or crude. Wasn't her lack of clear-cut endings cheating? And she was so edgy, pushing too many boundaries.

When she was starting out, her own children's school

refused to accept copies of a book of hers that she donated. Some schools even had a brochure called "How to Rid Your Schools and Libraries of Judy Blume Books." Students told her that if they wrote a report on one of her books, they'd get points taken off their grade.

Judy had to grow a thick skin and try not to be hurt, because at least the kids were reading her.

Eventually it stopped bothering her that some adults didn't want their children to read her books. Much more outrageous was that some people didn't want *any* kids to read them. They officially demanded that schools and libraries get her books off the shelves.

Besides being rude, wasn't this book banning unconstitutional? The Constitution protected Americans' freedom of speech and freedom of the press. Shouldn't kids be able to read what they wanted to?

Around 1980 the book banners felt free to join together and squelch her and her books. It got to the point where Judy, while writing, sometimes thought of taking out scenes or words people might object to. Her son would give her pep talks: "You're Judy Blume! You're known for being honest."

From 1982 to 1996 she was the most banned author in America.

For a people pleaser, this really hurt. She tried to take it in stride: "I pretend they're talking about someone else."

Then she decided to fight back. After all, breaking the rules was what she did: "But when you say to me, 'No, you can't do this,' I say, 'Oh yes, I can! . . . You can't tell me what to do.'"

But the problem was far bigger than her personal hurt feelings. She began speaking out to defend not just her books but anyone's. She talked to book banners directly or through interviews. She went on TV talk shows. She spoke at teachers' and librarians' conferences, worried that they would be afraid to share these books with their children. She gave out names and numbers of support groups to let them know they weren't alone.

The problem was fear, she believed. Fear of books can be contagious and carry chilling consequences. As Judy and others pointed out, no books would be left on the shelves if everyone could ban whatever they didn't like.

Judy believed that the answer was not "protecting" children from real life, but, rather, encouraging communication: "Let children read whatever they want, and then talk about it with them. If parents and kids can talk together, we won't have as much censorship, because we won't have as much fear."

In addition to being a superstar writer, she had become a fighter for the freedom to read.

Sometimes Judy realized she was singing to herself as she walked down a street. She always ended her school talks by saying, "I'm really happy being me. . . . I have no regrets. I just have lots of ideas!"

Her books total twenty-eight so far, including those written for adults. People around the world read them—her books have been translated into dozens of languages. A lot of people read them—her total sales top eighty million copies. A lot of award givers read her books too—Judy has won more than ninety awards. The ones that mean the most to her are the ones voted on by children themselves.

Fame did not go to her head: "My success was such a surprise. Such an absolute shocking surprise to me, to find out that this thing that you're sure you don't even know how to do speaks to so many people."

Her third marriage, to George Cooper, a former law professor, has been happy. She's close to her two children—Randy (an airline pilot, not a stewardess) and Larry (a filmmaker)—as well as to her stepdaughter, Amanda, and a grandson. She owns several houses. She has battled cancer twice, most recently in 2012.

Judy became a hero. She paved the way for other writers, especially women, to write much more frankly. Writers of edgy books today owe her a debt. Said one prominent writer: "It's kind of impossible to overstate how much what you do has made it possible for me and so many women I admire to make their work."

Some women have said that Judy Blume books saved their lives, and they still treasure her books as adults.

As much as she has been given, she gives back. Besides

her work on behalf of free speech, she is on the board of directors for the Authors Guild, a group that helps writers. She is a founding member of the Society of Children's Book Writers and Illustrators, an organization especially helpful to beginners.

Her books have stayed popular. The big subjects don't change, she pointed out: "It's always families, friendships, and schools."

Over the years she has received an unbelievable amount of mail from kids. So much that she needed assistants to handle as many as two thousand letters a month. Kids confided in her, asked for advice, and told their own stories.

For kids with serious problems, she turned to experts to get advice, pointing to all the resources that could help. Sometimes the responsibility was overwhelming, and Judy admitted to getting professional help herself to cope.

As a way of reaching as many kids as possible, she collected some of her letters into a book called *Letters to Judy: What Your Kids Wish They Could Tell You*. The most common theme was lack of communication between parents and children. Judy could relate, remembering her issues with her own mom: "I felt that I could never really please her."

Somehow Judy Blume and her books have remained timeless. "Everything around us changes," she says, "but the human condition doesn't change . . . the need for love and acceptance, and getting to know yourself and your place in the world."

To many kids, her books seemed to whisper, *You are not alone*.

Judy Blume's Books for Young Readers

The One in the Middle Is the Green Kangaroo (1969)

Iggie's House (1970)

Are You There God? It's Me, Margaret (1970)

Then Again, Maybe I Won't (1971)

Freckle Juice (1971)

It's Not the End of the World (1972)

Tales of a Fourth Grade Nothing (1972)

Otherwise Known as Sheila the Great (1972)

Deenie (1973)

Blubber (1974)

Starring Sally J. Freedman as Herself (1977)

Superfudge (1980)

The Pain and the Great One (1984)

Just as Long as We're Together (1987)

Fudge-a-Mania (1990)

Here's to You, Rachel Robinson (1993)

Double Fudge (2002)

Soupy Saturdays with the Pain and the Great One (2007)

Cool Zone with the Pain and the Great One (2008)

Going, Going, Gone! with the Pain and the Great One (2008)

Friend or Fiend? with the Pain and the Great One (2009)

★ SOURCES AND FURTHER READING ★

Books
(* especially for young readers)

Blume, Judy. *Letters to Judy: What Your Kids Wish They Could Tell You*. New York: Putnam, 1986.

Heti, Sheila, and Ross Simonini. *Judy Blume and Lena Dunham in Conversation*. San Francisco: McSweeney's, 2013.

* Lee, Betsy. *Judy Blume's Story*. New York: Dillon, 1981.

O'Connell, Jennifer. *Everything I Needed to Know About Being a Girl I Learned from Judy Blume*. New York: Simon & Schuster, 2007.

* Telford, Cee. *Judy Blume*. New York: Rosen, 2004.

Tracy, Kathleen A. *Judy Blume: A Biography*. Westport, CT: Greenwood, 2007.

Weidt, Maryann N. *Presenting Judy Blume*. New York: Dell, 1990.

* Wheeler, Jill C. *Judy Blume*. Edina, MN: ABDO, 2004.

Websites

American Booksellers Foundation for Free Expression: **www.abffe.org**

American Library Association Office for Intellectual Freedom: **www.ala.org/offices/oif**

Judy Blume Official Site: **www.judyblume.com**

Judy Blume on Facebook: **www.facebook.com/ItsMeJudyBlume**

Judy Blume on Twitter: **twitter.com/judyblume**

National Coalition Against Censorship: **www.ncac.org**

People for the American Way: **www.pfaw.org**

Society of Children's Book Writers and Illustrators: **www.scbwi.org**

★ INDEX ★